AMPHITRYON

After Kleist
by way of Molière
with a little bit of Giraudoux
thrown in

adapted by
Eric Overmyer

BROADWAY PLAY PUBLISHING INC
New York
www.broadwayplaypublishing.com
info@broadwayplaypublishing.com

AMPHITRYON

Cover photo by T Charles Erickson
Book design: Marie Donovan
Page make-up: Adobe Indesign
Typeface: Palatino

AMPHITRYON opened at the Classic Stage Company (David Esbjornson, Artistic Director; Patricia Taylor, Managing Director) in New York City, on 18 April 1995. The cast and creative contributors were as follows:

JUPITER.. Peter Francis James
MERCURY.. Arthur Hanket
ALCMENA ....Gina Torres
GODDESS OF NIGHT .... Katherine Leask
MR DAWN .... David Edward Jones
SOSIA.. Ken Cheeseman
CHARIS.. Katherine Leask
AMPHITRYON .... Michael James Reed
CAPTAIN .... David Edward Jones
COLONEL .... David Edward Jones

Director ....Brian Kulick
Scenic & costume design ....Mark Wendland
Lighting design .... Kevin Adams
Production stage manager .... Lisa Iacucci
Casting director ....Judy Dennis

ACKNOWLEDGMENTS

I am indebted to Brian Kulick and David Esbjornson for asking me to adapt Kleist's AMPHITRYON for the Classic Stage Company.

PROLOGUE

Scene One

(Olympus. A cloud. JUPITER *and* MERCURY, *lounging. Spying on a certain person down on Earth.)*

JUPITER: There she is!

MERCURY: Where?

JUPITER: That candlelit window—there!

MERCURY: There?

JUPITER: No. There! See?

MERCURY: Oh. Yes.

JUPITER: See her? See her pass by the window? Alcmena! Isn't she beautiful? Isn't her silhouette spectacular! Oh, how I flash and yearn! If only!

MERCURY: Listen, Jupiter, if you're in love with a mortal woman, why don't you just use your godlike faculties to woo her?

JUPITER: They're not god*like*. I *am* a god. I'm *father* of the gods—

MERCURY: Alright, why don't you use your god-*given*, if you're going to quibble, faculties, to woo her? Why not do as you've done so many times before? Transform yourself into a zephyr, flash to Earth, caress her with soft breezes, make love to her like the wind—

both figuratively and literally—and you're back home before anyone—especially Hera—is the wiser.

JUPITER: I'm bored with that routine.

MERCURY: You've got it down. No muss, no fuss, no morning-after recriminations. You have an entertaining afternoon, she has a pleasant dream, a most refreshing nap, and, nine months later, a very *bright*, precocious baby. *Way* ahead of the other kids. And the proud parents have no idea who the real father of this prodigy is. Doesn't take after anyone on *my* side of the family. Works out well for everyone. And—improves the gene pool.

JUPITER: I long for something more—visceral. I want to make love like human beings do. With all the attendant delights and difficulties.

MERCURY: Why? It's so messy. Emotional—

JUPITER: Sounds wonderful. Besides, you go down there and dally with mortal women on their own terms all the time.

MERCURY: It's true, I do. I like Earth. It's—so—fecund. It's the only world in the universe which smells exactly like a sweaty horse.

JUPITER: Really.

MERCURY: I love that.

JUPITER: *(Re:* ALCMENA*)* Isn't she beautiful?

MERCURY: Gorgeous. And faithful.

JUPITER: Faithful?

MERCURY: Absolutely.

JUPITER: Never falters?

MERCURY: Never. Even now, though her husband's been away at war for five long months.

JUPITER: Hmmm. What's his name?

MERCURY: Amphitryon.

JUPITER: Amphitryon. Five long months, did you say? In that case, I think she'd welcome a little visit from the gods.

MERCURY: Not Alcmena.

JUPITER: Certainly, she'd be more receptive—

MERCURY: Not her. She's steadfast. If you want her, you can't just waltz in there like you own the place—

JUPITER: But I do own the place! I do!

MERCURY: You have to try a more subtle approach.

JUPITER: What do you suggest?

MERCURY: Well, if you're not going to impersonate a zephyr, and she won't cheat on her husband, not even with you, Jupiter, father of all the gods—I guess you'll just have to *be* her husband, won't you?

JUPITER: What an excellent idea! And you shall be his servant, Sosia!

MERCURY: Sounds like fun. Since these sorts of deceptions are better done under cover of darkness, let me hurry and catch the Goddess of Night before she departs the general vicinity of greater metropolitan Thebes—

JUPITER: Wonderful! While you're taking care of that, I'll just go—*change.*

*(*JUPITER *leaves, as* MERCURY*—)*

Scene Two

(—descends from his cloud; the GODDESS OF NIGHT *enters.)*

MERCURY: A word with you, lovely Night!

GODDESS OF NIGHT: Oh, it's you! I'd love to stay and chat, but I'm running a little late. It's that damn full moon, it messes me up every month.

MERCURY: Do me a favor?

GODDESS OF NIGHT: Name it.

MERCURY: Look, can you see your way clear to linger over Thebes just a little bit longer this evening?

GODDESS OF NIGHT: Why?

MERCURY: Well, if you must know, it's—it's Jupiter.

GODDESS OF NIGHT: Don't tell me—

MERCURY: He's got a date.

GODDESS OF NIGHT: Really. What a surprise. With whom?

MERCURY: The lovely, talented, and faithful Alcmena, who's married to—

GODDESS OF NIGHT: And probably dreaming of this very moment—

MERCURY: Amphitryon—

GODDESS OF NIGHT: The general? Who even as we speak sleeps soundly in his battlefield tent, exhausted by his great victory over the vulgar Athenians, and dreaming in turn of his lovely wife, with no earthly idea of the heavenly mischief afoot?

MERCURY: The same.

GODDESS OF NIGHT: Jupiter, Jupiter, Jupiter. That god. You put him up to this, didn't you?

MERCURY: His idea. Swear. So, what do you say? Stay? Just a little bit longer?

GODDESS OF NIGHT: How much longer?

MERCURY: Who knows? A couple of hours, maybe more. He has no sense of time—

GODDESS OF NIGHT: That's certainly true. Once he gets going—

MERCURY: Tireless?

GODDESS OF NIGHT: Insatiable.

MERCURY: *(Interest piqued)* Really. You and he?

GODDESS OF NIGHT: *(Coy)* Once in a while. Eclipses, mostly.

MERCURY: I had no idea. Is he good?

GODDESS OF NIGHT: Are you kidding? They don't call him father of the gods for nothing, you know.

MERCURY: Interesting. Well?

GODDESS OF NIGHT: Oh, brother. What choice do I have?

MERCURY: You're a goddess. You won't regret it— *(He gives her a kiss and flies offstage.)*

GODDESS OF NIGHT: I already do. I hate this. These divine assignations wreak havoc with my timetable. What it does to high tide and low tide, you have no idea. Oh, well. I'll just have to make up the difference somewhere over the Mediterranean, I suppose. When somebody says, "Where does the time go?" now you know. It goes to celestial shenanigans like these.

*(*MR DAWN *enters, all rosy-fingered, sleepy, smoking a cigarette and drinking a blue-and-white paper cup of take-out coffee from a Greek deli, the slogan "It's Our Pleasure To Serve You" prominently displayed.* MR DAWN *yawns.)*

GODDESS OF NIGHT: Look. If it isn't rosy-fingered Dawn himself. Right on schedule.

MR DAWN: When am I not? You still here? I thought you'd be fading away by now. Looks like the middle of the night. I get the time wrong? What is it, daylight savings? They set the clocks back, or what?

GODDESS OF NIGHT: Jupiter. You know.

MR DAWN: Ah. Got it.

GODDESS OF NIGHT: You can go back to bed for a few hours. I'll call you when I need you—

MR DAWN: Fine by me.

*(*MR DAWN *shuffles off. The* GODDESS OF NIGHT *sighs, gestures, spreading some more darkness, and disappears as—)*

END OF PROLOGUE

ACT ONE

Scene One

(Night. Outside AMPHITRYON*'s palazzo in Thebes—which looks surprisingly like Venice.)*

(Carnival. The streets are full of masked revelers and musicians. SOSIA *enters, carrying a lantern. Watches suspiciously as a group of maskers goes by.)*

SOSIA: Highwaymen, probably. They may look like revelers to you, but to me—cutthroats, murderers, and thieves. Brigands, bandits, and buccaneers. Freebooting, swashbuckling, purse-cutting pirates. *(Shivers)* Brrrrr. What could my master be thinking of, sending me abroad in the dead of night, during carnival no less, when the whole world has license to misbehave. "Sosia," he said, in that *voice* of his, "my faithful servant, my family retainer, my omnipresent minion—" —which is how he talks— "Get you gone to Thebes, proclaim my great victory, shout it to the rooftops" —or from the rooftops, I can't remember which—" and alert my wife to my imminent arrival." "But, sir," I said, "it's dark out. Couldn't it wait 'til morning?" *(Looks at audience)* Apparently not. *(Looks behind—does take)* Our palazzo! Thank God, I'm home. A harrowing journey, let me tell you. I nearly lost my life a dozen times between the battlefield and blessed Thebes, my old hometown. Now, let's see. I'm supposed to give the lovely Alcmena a full and reliable report on her husband—that would be my master, Amphitryon—and his great victory over the vulgar Athenians. If only I'd been there. Actually, I *was* there, but I couldn't really see the battle from where I was—um—observing. I meant to poke my head out once or twice from the tent and take notes, but— *(Shrugs)* Okay, okay. I should've looked. But the spears, the arrows, flying hither and thither, this way and that, the swords, swoosh, swoosh, swish, the battle axes, chop, chop, swoosh, bash, crash, snicker snack—the whole thing was really just too chaotic to get mixed up with. I'll just make it up! Who would know the difference? I have the gift. It comes from my grandfather, who could embroider a trip to the market for a turnip into tales of brave Ulysses. *(Hears something)* Did you hear something? *(He looks around.)* Nothing. *(He hears something again. Looks around.)* There it is again. Just a minute. *(He walks away from the door momentarily, just as—)*

Scene Two

*(*MERCURY*, dressed as* SOSIA*, and to all eyes, except ours of course, looking exactly like* SOSIA*, comes out of* AMPHITRYON*'s palazzo.)*

MERCURY: *(Re:* SOSIA*)* Damn! The plot thickens. If I don't get this unexpected complication away from here, post haste, then all of our divine plans, namely Jupiter's scheme to take the very form of Amphitryon and lay—or is it lie—with his lovely wife, Alcmena—may go up in smoke. *(To audience)* May I introduce myself? I'm Mercury. *The* Mercury. You know, this penchant we Greek gods have for sleeping with mortal women is—peculiar, don't you think? I mean, what is this fatal flaw? Aren't goddesses good enough? It's a puzzlement.

SOSIA: *(Not seeing* MERCURY*)* I guess that noise was just a figment of my overactive imagination. *(He looks at his watch, shakes it to see if it's still running.)* You know, this seems to be a *very* long night indeed. Let's see, it was well after sunset when I set out, and it's a good five hours from the battlefield to Thebes— *(Looks at horizon)* Dawn should be breaking by now, but instead it's still the middle of the night. Perhaps I fell asleep in a drunken stupor and have somehow misplaced a whole day—god knows it's happened before—and it's now night once more. Or, perhaps something is amiss in the heavens—that's always possible—and the gods are goofing around again.

MERCURY: *(Aloud)* The gods? "Goofing around"? Oh, such disrespect. I'll have to teach this mere mortal a lesson in manners and humility. *(To* SOSIA*)* What rude hooligan disturbs my sleep?

SOSIA: *(Sees* MERCURY*—starts)* Oh, dear. Who's this ruffian? Courage. I'll just whistle a happy tune— *(He whistles weakly.)*

MERCURY: I suppose I'll have to thrash this thug within an inch of his worthless life—

SOSIA: Uh-oh. Doesn't seem to be much of a music lover.

MERCURY: *(Flexing)* It's been more than a week since I've thrashed anyone within an inch of his life. I feel rusty. I'm out of practice. I'm itching to regain my form.

SOSIA: You don't scare me, pretty boy. *(Aside)* Oh, my God. I'm paralyzed with fear. My knees are jelly. But maybe this *payaso* is just as frightened of me as I am of him. *(Aloud)* Don't press your luck, pal. See these? *(Brandishes one fist)* Six months in the hospital— *(Brandishes other fist)* —and sudden death! So, out of my way!

*(*MERCURY *blocks* SOSIA*'s way.)*

MERCURY: And who're you, may I ask?

SOSIA: I'm me. That's who.

MERCURY: And you are? Master or servant?

SOSIA: That all depends on how you look at it. Master to some, servant to others, you know how life is, it's a ladder—

MERCURY: You're a tramp, a vagabond, a worthless bum, a vagrant, a rapscalion, a rascal , and a stray dog—

SOSIA: You know, I'd love to stay here and have a full and frank exchange of views, and really work out our differences, but, as I said, I've got places to go and things to do, so—

*(*SOSIA *starts to go inside and once more* MERCURY *blocks his way.)*

MERCURY: Where are you off to? Tell me the truth. Spill the beans or suffer the consequences—

SOSIA: Well, since you insist. Through those doors.

MERCURY: What's your name again?

SOSIA: My name is Sosia. With an S.

MERCURY: Sosia? Sosia, you say?

SOSIA: Sosia, that's right. Sosia. Sosia, Sosia, Sosia.

MERCURY: I'm going to break every bone in your miserable body. How dare you appropriate the name of Sosia?

SOSIA: Excuse me? Appropriate? Oh, that really is the last straw. I'm sorry, but you, Sir, are laboring under a misapprehension. I did not appropriate my name, it was given to me. By my father. Whose name was also Sosia. As was his father's before him. I come from a long line of Sosias.

(MERCURY seizes SOSIA by the scruff.)

SOSIA: Help! Murder! Help! Citizens of Thebes! Stop your senseless carousing and revelry and merrymaking and help me! Help!

MERCURY: I don't think they can hear you, they're having much too good a time!

SOSIA: Let me go!

MERCURY: Then tell me who you are, and this time tell the truth.

SOSIA: *(Aside)* If I say I'm Sosia, he'll kill me. *(Aloud)* Okay, okay. I'm, uh, I'm, uh—

MERCURY: Are you still Sosia?

SOSIA: I'm—whoever you say I am.

MERCURY: You used to be Sosia.

SOSIA: So I did. I must admit that up until this very moment and for the last thirty-nine years or so I've been under that impression. But now—

MERCURY: Now—

SOSIA: Now I see I was mistaken. You've convinced me. I'd like to thank you for clearing up some three- or four-odd decades of misapprehension—

MERCURY: Good. Because my name is Sosia.

SOSIA: Excuse me?

MERCURY: Sosia. With an S.

SOSIA: You say you're Sosia?

MERCURY: So I say. How say you?

SOSIA: Can we talk?

MERCURY: Certainly.

(MERCURY releases SOSIA.)

SOSIA: How did you come up with this fantastic idea? Taking my name? I mean, my coat, my purse, even my chicken dinner. But my name? What can you do with it? You can't wear it. You can't hock it. What good does it do you?

MERCURY: I am Sosia. It is you who have taken my name.

SOSIA: *(To audience)* Am I dreaming? Perhaps I've fallen off my horse? Maybe I had one too many sips of plum brandy for breakfast. It's been known to happen. *(To* MERCURY*)* I could swear Amphitryon sent me here to tell his wife—my mistress Alcmena—about his great victory over the vulgar Athenians, and so on and so forth, at great length and with lots of colorful embroidery.

MERCURY: Exactly so. Except that Amphitryon sent me on that mission, not you. Because I am Sosia, his servant, son of a sailor—

SOSIA: Shepherd—

MERCURY: Shepherd, excuse me, and husband of that Charis, who drives me crazy with her caprices and whims and moods and extravangances—

SOSIA: Sounds like my little Charis, all right—

MERCURY: And I'm the same Sosia who recently spent some time in the hoosegow for a certain minor offense against public decency—

SOSIA: *(Aside)* Now, how does he know *that*? *(Looking at* MERCURY*)* You can't help but take him seriously, a little. I mean, he's even my height and build, just about, and dressed rather like me, now that I get a good look at him. He even has my smirk, god dammit! He's copied my expressions. I know. I'll ask him a couple of questions to which and to wit only I could know the answers. *(To* MERCURY*)* Now, Sirrah. About the booty—

MERCURY: Booty?

SOSIA: From the battle—

MERCURY: Ah. The booty from the battle.

SOSIA: Exactly so. What's the booty, and what does Amphitryon intend to do with it?

MERCURY: The booty happens to be the Athenian general's bejeweled head-band, which he intends to give to his lovely wife, Alcmena, as a token of his undying affection.

SOSIA: *(Aside)* Damn. *(To* MERCURY*)* And how is he presenting this priceless bauble to his beloved?

MERCURY: In a golden case, on which is stamped his personal coat-of-arms.

SOSIA: *(Aside)* Now, how on Earth does he know *that*? *(Looking at* MERCURY*)* He looks more like me every moment. I pinch myself— *(He does.)* I still feel like Sosia. But I grow more unsure of my own existence every moment. One more question only I could know. *(To* MERCURY*)* And what exactly were you doing, during the battle? Did you, for instance, distinguish yourself by feat of arms?

MERCURY: Hardly. I was hiding.

SOSIA: *(Aside)* Damn. *(To* MERCURY*)* I beg your pardon. Hiding? Did I hear you correctly? Hiding where?

MERCURY: In a tent.

SOSIA: *(Aside)* Damn, and double damn. *(To* MERCURY*)* And what were you doing in that tent? Besides hiding, I mean.

MERCURY: Devouring a smoked ham. And washing it down with a bottle of beer. Persian beer. Imported.

(At this revelation, SOSIA *faints dead away.* MERCURY *walks over and kneels down, and gives him a slap to revive him. He comes to, sees* MERCURY, *starts.)*

SOSIA: I give up. You are Sosia. As for me, I have no idea who I am.

MERCURY: When I'm done being you, you can go back to being you, but until then, don't you dare be you, on pain of death. Understand me?

SOSIA: Okay, okay. I'll lay low and be someone else, until this all blows over. Farewell.

*(*SOSIA *scrambles to his feet and starts into the house.* MERCURY *grabs him.)*

MERCURY: What are you, hard of hearing? Didn't I just threaten your life?

*(*MERCURY *begins to cuff* SOSIA, *who dodges the blows.)*

SOSIA: Sorry! Sorry! Force of habit. When you've gone in the same entrance all your life, it's hard to turn one's back on hearth and home and spouse and a hot meal and trot off in a different direction. But don't worry, I'll just slink off into the night like a thief, and hope that I awake soon from this unbearable dream. *(He goes.)*

Scene Three

*(*MERCURY, *alone)*

MERCURY: Finally. What a stubborn fellow. He might have spared himself some nasty blows. No doubt his ears are still ringing. He has no idea he just got a thrashing from a god. I should have told him. It would have made him feel better. It's an honor, really, to be mauled by one of the immortals. I just hope all this commotion and carrying on didn't wake the lovers. Ah, but here they come now.

Scene Four

*(*JUPITER*, looking to all the world [except us] exactly like* AMPHITRYON*, enters, followed by a radiant* ALCMENA*, and her serving woman,* CHARIS*.)*

ALCMENA: Amphitryon, must you go? You just got here, my darling.

JUPITER: I have seized these tender moments unbeknownst to anyone, my dearest, and now I must return to my military post. *(He kisses her fiercely, then solemnly gives her the jeweled head-band.)* Treasure this—bauble.

ALCMENA: I would gladly trade this booty seized in battle for a simple bouquet of violets—or forsythia, perhaps, for forsythia is my favorite, absolutely—gathered myself from outside the door of our modest rustic white-washed retirement cottage on a small plot of land with perhaps a little grove of olive trees and a few goats. We need no one and nothing else, my darling—just the two of us. I know you love the cheering crowds, the acclaim of poets, the adulation of multitudes. And so do I darling. For you belong to me, and your successes fill me with a sweet sweet feeling. But all of that sweet feeling evaporates when I think of you in battle, when I imagine an enemy's arrow aimed at your breast, a vulgar Athenian sword pointed at your throat. Then that sweet feeling curdles in my breast and becomes bleak despair.

JUPITER: You mustn't worry. Believe me, I am impervious to arrows and swords of any sort. Take my word for it.

ALCMENA: But, Darling, how can that be? You are mortal, are you not?

JUPITER: Well—

ALCMENA: Don't get too cocky, Darling. Besides, the palazzo is so empty when you're gone. And the hours so dull. And the days drag on. I did not realize what Thebes has stolen from me until today, my darling, when you were mine again for two short hours.

JUPITER: They were too short, weren't they, those two short hours. You are delightful, my darling. But tell me something. The man you received today in your bridal bed—

ALCMENA: Yes?

JUPITER: Was he your beloved, or merely your spouse?

ALCMENA: What sort of riddle is this? He was both! My husband and my lover!

JUPITER: Alcmena, my darling, my feelings for you so far outstrip mere matrimony, I would rather you would make a distinction between the two, and consider me your beloved—and not your husband, the vain and arrogant general of Thebes, who so recently wooed and won—undeservedly in my opinion—a beautiful and wealthy princess—i.e., your own sweet self. Give him your virtue—and keep all your love for me.

ALCMENA: Amphitryon, listen to you. The way you talk, people might think you were someone else, I don't know who. You may make these distinctions between husband and lover, but since the gods have given me both in your divine form, I hereby forgive the one for any crimes the other may have committed. There. Feel better?

JUPITER: Then promise me you will never forget the joys of this evening. Promise not to confuse these few precious hours we have spent together this night with the humdrum day-to-day domestic life of marriage—

ALCMENA: My darling, how could I confuse my humdrum household hours with what has just transpired between us? Tonight, beloved, you were like—a god.

JUPITER: I was, wasn't I?

ALCMENA: Oh, yes, you were.

JUPITER: Don't forget—

ALCMENA: How could I?

JUPITER: Promise—

ALCMENA: I promise—

JUPITER: And promise to think of me often once Amphitryon the general returns home for good from the war.

ALCMENA: You are acting so strangely, my darling. But of course, of course I'll think of you when you are home from the war for good.

JUPITER: Think of me the way I was tonight—

ALCMENA: The way you were tonight.

*(*JUPITER *kisses* ALCMENA *fiercely once again.)*

JUPITER: Thank you. Thank you. That means more to me than I can say. Farewell, my lovely. Duty calls.

ALCMENA: Amphitryon. Must you go? Really? Really, really, really? At least stay until dawn. The night must be almost over.

JUPITER: Tell me, Darling. Hasn't this evening gone by in a flash?

ALCMENA: Oh, yes. How time flies when I'm with you, my dearest.

JUPITER: For me too. Farewell. And rest assured I'll do my best to see that until we meet again, the nights we spend apart will be not a second longer than the Earth itself needs to make its way through the tempestuous heavens.

(JUPITER *exits.* ALCMENA *looks after him, fondly.)*

ALCMENA: I have no idea what he's talking about. He's drunk. On love. And so am I. *(She giggles and goes off—)*

Scene Five

(—leaving MERCURY *and* CHARIS *alone onstage.)*

CHARIS: *(Aside)* Now that's what I call happily married. Husband and wife, after a long separation, can't keep their hands off each other. But that—lump—over there that I have the misfortune to be married to—he's about as tender as a tree stump.

MERCURY: *(Aside)* Now I must hurry and tell the Goddess of Night, who's already been cooling her heels over Thebes for seventeen long hours, while Jupiter's had his way with Alcmena, to make way for the dawn. It's high time she went on and cast her dark spell over other human misadventures. Besides, people just down the road from Thebes and over the next hill must be getting awfully tired of waiting for night to fall. Let's face it, Jupiter gets a glint in his eye and the celestial schedule goes all to hell.

(MERCURY *starts out.* CHARIS *snorts.)*

CHARIS: There he goes. My loving husband. *(Calls)* Oh, Sosia. Where do you think you're going?

MERCURY: What am I supposed to do? Shouldn't I be with Amphitryon? My Lord and Master?

CHARIS: You could at least say something to me. By way of greeting. Some little sweet nothing. I am your wife, after all, whom you haven't seen in some time, I might add. Or have you forgotten?

MERCURY: Not now. I don't have time for endearments. Besides, I've said it all before. Just—cast your memory back and choose something appropriate to the occasion. One of my better bon mots.

CHARIS: You're a jerk. I haven't seen you for weeks. You should be whispering tender valentines in my ear.

MERCURY: Like what?

CHARIS: Like dear sweet lovely sexy charming adorable precious little wife of mine without whom I cannot possibly live without, and so on and so forth, I've missed you so, I can't think of anyone but you— *(Looks at him)* Come on. Say something. Make an effort, it won't kill you.

MERCURY: Why? We've been married for a dozen years—

CHARIS: It seems like two—

MERCURY: Only two?

CHARIS: Two dozen—

MERCURY: To be frank, Darling, I ran out of fresh endearments halfway through the honeymoon.

CHARIS: Oh, you. You're worse than usual. You should be ashamed that Amphitryon, a great lord and general, who has vulgar Athenians to contend with and a whole army to run, is so much more tender in his love and submission to his wife than you are.

MERCURY: He's a newlywed, it hardly counts. If we were to act like that in public, middle-aged married couple that we are, they'd lock us up.

CHARIS: Did I not go and fix myself up and put on my face and change my clothes and make myself presentable as soon as you arrived? And all for naught, apparently.

MERCURY: You don't need to put on your face for me—

CHARIS: *(Tenderly)* Oh, Sosia—

MERCURY: Because it makes absolutely no difference, as far as I'm concerned. No matter what, we're just a boring old married couple, and our days of passion are behind us.

CHARIS: Oh, you! You are the limit! You don't deserve a wife like me. Faithful, upstanding, virtuous—

MERCURY: I wish you'd be a little less upstanding and a little more content. You wear me out with your constant carping and complaining—

CHARIS: So you don't care that I've been faithful to you all these years, that I've maintained my good name, that my reputation as a virtuous wife is still intact?

MERCURY: I guess I care. But why do you have to talk about it all the time?

CHARIS: You—no-goodnik! You deserve a wife who has a character like yours, who'll deceive you behind your back day and night like you do me.

MERCURY: When have I ever?

CHARIS: Every chance you get. Maybe I'll just give you what you deserve.

MERCURY: That'll be the day. I'm not worried about you.

CHARIS: Is that a dare? Should I take up with one of the many handsome, virile, young men who importune me every morning in the marketplace? Who practically beg for my favors? Who'd risk everything if I'd only see fit to bestow on them just a few of my abundant charms? Who pine away in hopeless and heretofore unrequited love?

MERCURY: Yes. Go ahead. Do what you like. Bestow your charms on every mug in the market. See if I care. Just don't tell me about it, alright? Spare me the tedious details, that's all I ask. Besides, a little consensual sin is a lot better for the body politic than a boatload of boring civic virtue. I personally think Thebes needs less honor and more peace. So long. I'm off to catch up with Amphitryon, who must be halfway back to camp by now. *(He leaves.)*

CHARIS: Ooo, that man! I wish I could pay him back in his own coin. I'd love to punish him. It won't be easy. How I regret my hard-won iron-clad reputation for virtue. Damn. *(She leaves.)*

END OF ACT ONE

ACT TWO

Scene One

*(*MERCURY *is onstage with* MR DAWN *as dawn breaks—with a rush, as the* GODDESS OF NIGHT *takes off in a hurry, like a jumbo jet.* MERCURY *waves goodbye to* GODDESS OF NIGHT, *takes a puff off* MR DAWN*'s cigarette, and exits.* MR DAWN *yawns and exits.* AMPHITRYON *and* SOSIA *enter.* AMPHITRYON *is in a, well—state. He's fit to be tied. He's having a cow.)*

AMPHITRYON: You expect me to believe this outlandish tale? I ought to have you hanged. At the very least, horsewhipped.

SOSIA: In that case, I'll keep my mouth shut. I must have been dreaming, Sir—or drunk.

AMPHITRYON: Yes, you must've been. To think I'd swallow such a fairy tale. The kind nannies spin at bedtime to summon the sandman for restless children.

SOSIA: *(Surprised)* Really, Sir? A tale like this?

AMPHITRYON: Well, some nannies. Progressive households. Never mind that. Tell me again. I must have the whole outlandish story straight before I set foot in my palazzo.

SOSIA: Alright, Sir, but please restrain yourself. You mustn't pop a gasket.

AMPHITRYON: I'll try.

SOSIA: I hate when the veins stand out on your forehead—

AMPHITRYON: *Alright.*

SOSIA: You want the truth, the whole truth, and nothing but the truth—or shall I sugarcoat it for you like they do in court?

AMPHITRYON: The truth. All of it. Every bit. Answer my questions.

SOSIA: Okay. Fire away.

AMPHITRYON: You came straight here, as I told you—

SOSIA: And a harrowing journey it was, Sir.

AMPHITRYON: You didn't stop to have a drink at some tavern along the way—

SOSIA: No, Sir, you expressly forbade me stop for any reason, especially that one.

AMPHITRYON: So I did. And then?

SOSIA: I attempted to enter our palazzo. But my way was barred.

AMPHITRYON: Barred? By whom?

SOSIA: *(He looks around, eyes wide, then whispers:)* Sosia.

AMPHITRYON: Sosia.

SOSIA: Sosia.

AMPHITRYON: *Some other* good-for-nothing, bound for a bad end, a day late and a dollar short, *Sosia*? Here in Thebes? I'm sure I would have heard of such a remarkable coincidence. How could there be two such Sosias in a city as small as Thebes? So which Sosia was this?

SOSIA: The same Sosia you yourself sent from camp and charged with coming here to your palazzo to tell your wife of your great victory over the vulgar Athenians.

AMPHITRYON: Oh. *That* Sosia.

SOSIA: That's the one. The same Sosia who knows all about the booty seized in battle, and the golden case sealed with your coat-of-arms, which you are going to give to your wife and which I have here in my possession.

AMPHITRYON: But that Sosia would be—you.

SOSIA: Me, Sire. That is to say, the me who arrived ahead of me and was already here when the me who is me arrived. Here.

AMPHITRYON: Do you actually believe this nonsense? This gobbledegook? Or this your idea of a joke? And will you still find it funny when you're swinging from the gallows?

SOSIA: I'm serious, Sir. I swear to you that I set out from camp for Thebes, a single Sosia, as there has been all my life, so far as I knew, and upon my arrival met myself, who came out of your palazzo, all refreshed and refurbished and full of piss and vinegar, and stared me in the eye, and threatened my well-being, and promised me bodily harm if I did not cease and desist being me immediately, and drove me back to camp in a state of considerable confusion. Sir.

AMPHITRYON: I must be the most mild-mannered general anywhere—

SOSIA: Yes, Sir—

AMPHITRYON: To put up with such doubletalk from a squirrelly servant like yourself—

SOSIA: Without a doubt, Sir, and if my tale annoys, please, let's talk of something else, something more pleasant. What are you giving up for Lent, Sir? Me, I think I'll give up lamb with mint sauce—

AMPHITRYON: Be quiet and let me think. And when have you ever had lamb with mint sauce?

SOSIA: Never, Sir, but I saw it once depicted in a painting, and the sheer succulence of the image has haunted me ever since—

AMPHITRYON: Is there more to your story?

SOSIA: Not much, but I can make it last for hours, if you like—

AMPHITRYON: Be brief, and help me make sense of it, that's all I ask.

SOSIA: I'm not sure I can do that, Sir. I'm not sure any man can do that. It *is* a fairy tale, spun from sunlight and moonbeams—and just as true, and just as hard to grasp.

AMPHITRYON: This other Sosia—the same as you in every way?

SOSIA: Two drops of water could not be more alike. Two snowflakes, two grains of sand, two peas in a pod, two mashed potatoes—

AMPHITRYON: Stop, stop, I understand the simile. But tell me, did you ever enter the palazzo and speak to my wife?

SOSIA: No, Sir! I did not!

AMPHITRYON: You scoundrel! That was your mission! Why not?

SOSIA: As I may have mentioned, Sir, before I could enter the palazzo I was thrashed soundly about the head and shoulders—

AMPHITRYON: By?

SOSIA: By me, Sir.

AMPHITRYON: You?

SOSIA: Not the me who's standing here before you, but the other me, who came out of the palazzo, the me who was here before the me who is here now ever got here—

AMPHITRYON: Come, let's go in. I can't listen to any more of this raving. But, wait! Here comes Alcmena.

SOSIA: With Charis, my own dear ball and chain, better half, lawfully wedded, 'til death do us part—

AMPHITRYON: Put a cork in it, will you? *(Re:* ALCMENA*)* She'll be pleasantly surprised, she's not expecting me this morning.

SOSIA: Nor is mine, I'll wager, although pleasantly surprised isn't the phrase I'd use to describe the look she usually has on her face when she sees me come through the door, taken aback is more like it—

AMPHITRYON: Shhh!

*(*AMPHITRYON *and* SOSIA *step back.)*

Scene Two

*(*ALCMENA *and* CHARIS *enter.)*

ALCMENA: Come, Charis. Let's go make an offering to the gods, to keep my husband safe—

CHARIS: Fine by me. And while we're at it, and speaking of husbands, why don't we make mine the offering? I'd be more than happy to sacrifice him to the gods for your sake—

SOSIA: You see how she pines for me when I'm away.

ALCMENA: *(Sees* AMPHITRYON*)* Amphitryon!

AMPHITRYON: Alcmena!

CHARIS: Sosia!

SOSIA: Charis!

CHARIS: What are you doing here?

ALCMENA: Back so soon?

CHARIS: We've hardly had time to miss you.

SOSIA: So I see.

AMPHITRYON: This is not exactly the tender reception I anticipated. "Back so soon?"I thought you'd be overjoyed to see me, Darling, since I've been gone so long.

ALCMENA: And I do miss you every moment we're apart. I'm sorry, Darling, it's just that I did not expect to see you this morning, you've taken me by surprise—

AMPHITRYON: It's I who must apologize, Darling. I sent my faithful servant Sosia on ahead yesterday to inform you of my imminent arrival, and clearly he failed to carry out his task. I suppose the five long months I've been away at war have passed like five minutes here in Thebes, occupied as you've been with your usual pleasures, and lately consumed no doubt by the caprices of Carnival.

ALCMENA: On the contrary, Darling, your servant did appear—

CHARIS: It's true, Sir, he did.

ALCMENA: —to announce your arrival—which occurred shortly thereafter, as you must remember, at twilight—

CHARIS: On the button—

ALCMENA: And I greeted you with open arms and overflowing heart and tons of kisses—

CHARIS: As heart-warming a public display of marital affection as you'll ever want to see, Sir, you set a good example. *(To* SOSIA*)* I hope you were paying attention.

ALCMENA: And whence we commenced to retire to our bed and spend the rest of the night in vigorous and joyful lovemaking. And if that was insufficient, forgive me, Darling, but I believe I gave you all I had to give, and more, at that moment, although now, the miracle of love being what it is, renewable as the spring and akin to the ever-brimming and always replenished goblet from which mighty Ulysses drank to prove his valor— *(Flirting)* I could easily find myself in the mood once more, my darling, if you are so inclined—

AMPHITRYON: *(Interrupting her)* If memory serves, Darling, that was Thor, not Ulyssess, with the ever-brimming goblet, and you've confused your Greek myths with your Norse, but no matter, never mind. But what's this about greeting me with open arms and tons of kisses and an ardent heart? Not to mention a night-long bout of joyful—

ALCMENA: And vigorous—

AMPHITRYON: *(Gritting his teeth) Vigorous*—lovemaking.

ALCMENA: Have you forgotten last night? How I came to you? How I did everything you asked and more? How the room spun? How the earth moved?

AMPHITRYON: What are you saying?

ALCMENA: That I had never—as I told you, and more than amply demonstrated all night long—experienced such joy, such transports of physical ecstacy, such sheer connubial bliss—

AMPHITRYON: Indeed—

ALCMENA: —and you swore the same.

AMPHITRYON: I did?

ALCMENA: In fact, you swore a solemn oath that Hera herself had never so delighted Jupiter. Which was a very sweet thing to say, Darling, and quite flattering.

AMPHITRYON: I'll be damned!

ALCMENA: And then, as dawn was breaking, you stole away, I could not hold you, though I begged and pleaded for you please to come back to bed. And then I slept, briefly, utterly and joyfully exhausted, and just now got up from my marriage bed, just moments ago, in fact, a smile on my lips and roses in my cheeks, and was on my way to the temple to make an offering to the gods for your protection—

CHARIS: It's true, Sir, she was—

ALCMENA: And here I come upon you in the street, unexpectedly returned and feigning forgetfulness of last night. Fishing for compliments, I suppose, you vain man—

AMPHITRYON: Perhaps you had a dream, Alcmena—

ALCMENA: That was no dream, Amphitryon—

AMPHITRYON: That foreshadowed my return to you.

ALCMENA: Are you serious? You really don't remember last night?

AMPHITRYON: I remember last night, but nothing of what you describe.

ALCMENA: Have you been robbed of your memory? Are you suffering from amnesia? Do you mock my wifely love?

AMPHITRYON: Do you mean to tell me—let me see if I have this right—that I stole in here at twilight yesterday and kissed you?

ALCMENA: *Kissed* me? *KISSED* me? You permitted yourself every pleasure and liberty that a husband may expect from an eager and consensual wife—

AMPHITRYON: Every—pleasure—and liberty?

ALCMENA: Given more than willingly and returned twicefold—

AMPHITRYON: Oh, my god. My head is spinning.

ALCMENA: Do you deny it? That you were here, yesterday, in the palazzo, in our bedroom, in my arms?

AMPHITRYON: I do.

ALCMENA: Oh, Amphitryon! Why do you seek to hurt me so?

AMPHITRYON: Where are your witnesses?

CHARIS: I for one, Sir.

ALCMENA: The whole household saw you arrive. The rest of the servants, too. Including— *(Re:* SOSIA*)* yours.

CHARIS: Well? Speak up, Sirrah!

SOSIA: It's—complicated.

CHARIS: But you were here.

SOSIA: More than once. But at the present time I'm unwilling to swear to much of anything—

CHARIS: Oh, boy. What a stalwart fellow.

ALCMENA: Not to mention all the other servants. And even the dogs, who wagged their tails so happily to see you.

AMPHITRYON: Impossible. I was in camp all evening, some five hours from Thebes, writing my memoirs. I have only just arrived. This is the first time in five months I have set sandal on these cobblestone streets.

*(*ALCMENA *holds up the jewel* JUPITER *gave her.)*

ALCMENA: If you weren't here, then where did I get this? This—booty.

SOSIA: Good question.

AMPHITRYON: The booty! From the battle! And how did you come by that?

ALCMENA: From your hand.

AMPHITRYON: Already? But that's not possible—

ALCMENA: You said you captured it in battle.

AMPHITRYON: I did, but—

ALCMENA: Have you changed your mind? Do you want it back?

AMPHITRYON: No, I intended for you to have it, but—

SOSIA: I'll settle this. *(He brings forth a small golden case.)* Here's the case my master gave me which I was supposed to deliver to you, my lady, but could not, owing to circumstances too impossible to explain—

AMPHITRYON: Get on with it.

SOSIA: Yes, Sir. You see? *(Holds it up)* The seal's not yet broken. *(Breaking it)* I'll just break it— *(He opens the case. He's stunned. It's empty.)* It's empty.

AMPHITRYON: What have the gods done to me?

SOSIA: Same as to me, Master. They've doubled you. Amphitryon was here before, it's obvious—

ALCMENA: *(To* AMPHITRYON*)* Will you go on denying that last evening you came to me, and I rewarded your valor—both on the battlefield and in the bedroom—to the best of my abilities?

AMPHITRYON: No.

ALCMENA: Thank god.

CHARIS: He's coming around, at last.

AMPHITRYON: But humor me, Darling. Tell me exactly what went on last night while I was in the palazzo.

ALCMENA: Oh, I get it. You are fishing for compliments, aren't you? Just as I suggested. Not content with hearing me call your name to heaven over and over while we made love, or showering you with compliments after, or singing your praises to anyone who will listen, without a shred of matronly modesty or shame? Very well, if you are so hungry for accolades from your wife—

AMPHITRYON: No, no, it's not that. It's just that the memory of last night is not as—sharp as I would wish it.

ALCMENA: You're not ill, are you?

AMPHITRYON: No, no—

ALCMENA: You weren't struck in the head upon returning to the battlefield?

AMPHITRYON: Noooo—

ALCMENA: It distresses me no end, this peculiar amnesia of yours—

AMPHITRYON: Actually, Darling, I remember last night perfectly. I merely wish—before we go into the palazzo—to—relive—every—exciting—moment—in *excruciating* detail—

ALCMENA: Very well. If it pleases you, it pleases me. Charis? Will you provide the preamble?

CHARIS: Certainly, Mistress. Well, to make a long story short, and because I have biscuits baking in the oven, and a nice little risotto planned for lunch, I'll give you the condensed version. There was a great ruckus at the gates, I came out, your lordship was there in all his splendor, just as my worthless, no-good husband said you'd be, you wiped your feet and came in, took off your cloak, put your helmet on the sidetable, the dogs were barking, the servants were cheering, your lovely wife came running—

ALCMENA: I was spinning silk in the upstairs sitting room—

CHARIS: —you told us the whole story of your great victory over the vulgar Athenians, a blow-by-blow account which to these ears, although colorful, could have benefited by a little judicious editing, you then gave your wife the booty seized in battle, which she has now in her hand for all the world to see, and let me say, Sir, those are some swell stones, you're the kind of husband every girl dreams about, and I've been calling her Ladyship Miss Gotrocks all morning, and if other husbands who shall remain nameless knew what was good for them they'd get their fat butts out on the battlefield and pick up some booty for *their* wives instead of cowering in a tent and stuffing their faces with purloined pork products, but that's another matter, I digress, and then your wife gave you a big wet one in front of the gods and everybody, and we all cheered to see such matrimonial affection pass between the two of you, and then you both got up from the table in a great haste to go upstairs, and to the general merriment and rude commentary of the assembled multitude.

AMPHITRYON: And then what happened?

ALCMENA: We went upstairs, Darling.

AMPHITRYON: And?

ALCMENA: You know very well what happened then. You made love to me like a god! All night long!

(AMPHITRYON *staggers to his knees.)*

AMPHITRYON: These words are a dagger to my heart! O faithless wife! Whoever stole into your bed last evening at twilight was an imposter!

ALCMENA: An imposter?

AMPHITRYON: An imposter! Posing as Amphitryon!

ALCMENA: What outrageous rubbish!

AMPHITRYON: You are an adulteress!

ALCMENA: You are a bastard!

AMPHITRYON: Farewell to love! Farewell to happiness! Farewell to hope! From now on I'll revel in fury and revenge!

ALCMENA: Farewell to you, faithless husband. If you now love another, you should have told me straight out, instead of reverting to this convoluted conceit! Cowering like a—like a little—

CHARIS: Coward?

ALCMENA: Thank you—like a little coward behind the petticoats of this absurd story! This—this—this *dastardly* tale! This—this—*charade*! And you know how I hate charades! Before the day is over, you shall be free, Sir, of the matrimonial tie you obviously find so odious.

AMPHITRYON: Considering how publicly you have besmirched my honor—a divorce is the least of my demands. Although a grand deception has been perpetrated upon me, my mind does not yet grasp every angle of this conspiracy. What we need is a trial.

ALCMENA: A trial? Fine!

AMPHITRYON: Call your witnesses, and I'll call mine, including the whole Theban army, who will swear I did not stir out of my tent until early this morning. Then we'll get to the bottom of this, Madame, and you'll rue the day you deceived me—whether by malignant intent or from sheer gullibility—you and your spurious Amphitryon lover both!

ALCMENA: Fine, Sir. Gather your evidence, and I will gather mine. And we will see whose reputation remains intact!

AMPHITRYON: Madame—

ALCMENA: Sir—

SOSIA: Shall I—

AMPHITRYON: Silence! Not another word! *(He storms off.)*

CHARIS: My Lady, would you like me to—

ALCMENA: Quiet! I want to be alone! *(She storms into the house, leaving—)*

Scene Three

*(*CHARIS *and* SOSIA *together)*

CHARIS: I think the honeymoon is over. Is he nuts, or what, to think that he can get away with a story like that? Well, we'll clear this up once the witnesses arrive.

SOSIA: *(Aside)* I think I'm onto something here. My master and I, we've both been doubled somehow, it seems. *(Glances at* CHARIS*)* Oh, Dear—

CHARIS: *(Aside)* Look at him. He has the nerve to turn his back on me twice in twenty-four hours—

SOSIA: *(Aside)* I'm tempted to just forget the whole thing. I'd rather not know, truthfully. But, I suppose I have to ask. *(Clears his throat)* Oh, Charis, dearest—

CHARIS: Excuse me? I thought I heard a crow cough. Or perhaps it was maybe just the belch of a lonely bullfrog—

SOSIA: Good morning. Darling.

CHARIS: Oh, it's you. And you dare speak to me in those tones—

SOSIA: What tones? These are perfectly civil tones. Good morning, how are you, that's just the way it's done in civilized society. Why are you so angry over nothing?

CHARIS: Nothing? You call this nothing?

SOSIA: Well, yeah, sure, I mean, nothing means nothing, or at least, nothing much, so it seems to me if you're angry over the way I said good morning, I'd call that pretty close to nothing at all.

CHARIS: *(Furious)* I don't know why I don't just scratch your eyes out. Tell me why I don't.

SOSIA: *(Cringing)* Because you have no reason?

CHARIS: No reason? NO REASON? You call the shameless way you treated me earlier no reason?

SOSIA: How did I treat you? What happened? Tell me everything.

CHARIS: Oh, now I suppose, you'll claim, just like your master, that you weren't even here, that some other Sosia took your place—

SOSIA: Well, as a matter of fact—

CHARIS: Don't even think about it. You tell me a whopper like that, I'll serve you your own head pickled and on a platter.

SOSIA: The truth is, Darling, we were sold some Satanic beverage that erased our memory—

CHARIS: Oh, don't hand me that old song and dance about a Satanic beverage blackout, it just won't wash.

SOSIA: Honestly—

CHARIS: You really expect me to believe that you don't know how you behaved last night?

SOSIA: I don't, swear, scout's honor, cross my heart and hope to be a vulgar Athenian, I don't. Tell me. I can take it. If I've done wrong, I'll condemn myself.

CHARIS: Oh, I'm sure.

SOSIA: Tell me how I behaved.

CHARIS: You behaved despicably.

SOSIA: That goes without saying. Could you be a little more specific?

CHARIS: Oh, I think I can. Well, as you know, it was after midnight when you arrived, and the young couple had long since gone to bed, and you didn't even bother to so much as show your face in your own rooms, and so finally your wife, to her everlasting shame, actually had to go and hunt you down, and this after a five-month absence and not so much as a postcard, and there I found you snoring in the hallway outside their bedroom, and when I very tenderly woke you with a light blow on the noggin, and said come to bed, *dearest*, you said you had to remain at your post in case Amphitryon decided to leave Thebes unexpectedly in the middle of the night, a likely story, and moreover not one kind word or tender endearment did you mutter to me, and when I bent to kiss you, you turned your face to the wall and told me to leave you alone and let you sleep.

SOSIA: And you should thank your lucky stars I did just that—

CHARIS: Oh? And why is that?

SOSIA: Because I'd had garlic and pesto for supper—

CHARIS: Oh, don't give me that, so had I. And if last night wasn't bad enough, the way you treated me this morning really split the sheets between us as far as I'm concerned, and I swear on my unsullied reputation, you'll regret you ever gave me license to have you-know-what—

SOSIA: No, what? What license? I gave you license to—?

CHARIS: To have an affair.

SOSIA: No. I didn't.

CHARIS: Yes, you did. With one of the countless muscular sweaty virile Theban youths who are always after me at the market. Poor boys are practically wasting away with unrequited love. It's a tragedy, really.

SOSIA: It must have been some other jackass who said that, not me— *(Off her reaction)* All joking aside, I hope you won't take that remark seriously—

CHARIS: Now that you've planted the idea in my head, how can I help myself?

SOSIA: Let's talk about this later. Here comes Alcmena.

*(*CHARIS *and* SOSIA *compose themselves as—)*

Scene Four

*(—*ALCMENA *enters.)*

ALCMENA: Oh, Charis, what has happened to me? Last night I was the happiest of women, and today— today I'm miserable. Look at this jewel— *(She shows her* AMPHITRYON*'s gift.)* His monogram carved on the back—

CHARIS: That's not Amphitryon's monogram—

ALCMENA: Why, yes, it is—

CHARIS: No, it's not.

ALCMENA: That's an A, engraved in gold—

CHARIS: I don't think so. That's a J.

ALCMENA: A J?

CHARIS: A J.

ALCMENA: *(Swooning)* Gaslight—

CHARIS: My lady, tell me, what is it that so upsets you about the letter J?

ALCMENA: How can I explain the inexplicable? I went back to my room, uncertain if I'm awake or dreaming, my mind spinning with the crazy notion that perhaps I did indeed spend the night with another man, Amphitryon's impassioned, angry words still ringing in my ears, and I asked myself, could I be wrong?

CHARIS: How could you be wrong? Don't you know who you spent the night with?

ALCMENA: One of us must be wrong. For when I thought about it, I realized there was my husband, Amphitryon, slandering my husband, Amphitryon. And then I found the jewel and thought, this is solid evidence I can cling to—

CHARIS: But?

ALCMENA: But when I turned it over and brought the precious monogram to my lips to kiss it, over and over and over again, I thought—

CHARIS: Yes?

ALCMENA: That's not an A at all, it's a J. I stood there thunderstruck.

CHARIS: Oh, dear—

ALCMENA: And when you confirmed my worst fears—

CHARIS: Oh, I'm sure I'm wrong, that's probably an A after all. Let me see it again— *(Examines jewel)* I think that's an A, no question. A strange A, to be sure, an unfinished A, perhaps, or a nouveau A, but nonetheless an A. You just have to look at it the right way. Turn it just so. Catch the light. Squint. I see an A, don't you? Calm down. Everything will turn out alright.

ALCMENA: What makes you think so?

CHARIS: I don't know. Abject optimism?

ALCMENA: Oh, Charis! I'd rather be mistaken about myself than about my dear Amphitryon. I'd rather wake up some morning and find myself a Persian, or worse, a vulgar Athenian. Isn't this my hand? My nose? My bosom? My reflection in the mirror? Pluck out my eyes, like that dreary Oedipus, I'd still see my husband. Cut off my ears, cut out my tongue, take my touch and smell and all my senses away from me, and leave me but my heart, and I'd need no more than that to find him anywhere in the whole wide world.

CHARIS: Of course, my Lady. How could a woman be wrong about such a thing? You might mistake someone else's dress or pair of shoes, or even an eggbeater, for your own, and take them home—but a husband? You'd know your husband in the dark, and that's a fact. Besides, didn't we all see him? The whole palazzo staff, plus dogs, and in broad daylight, no less.

ALCMENA: *(Looking at jewel)* But still, there is the problem of this curious initial. It's clearly a J, no mistake about it—

CHARIS: Okay, it's a J—

ALCMENA: —but why didn't I notice that last night?

CHARIS: You were excited—

ALCMENA: I *was* excited. Amphitryon was so beautiful, so much himself he seemed to shine. He was like a painting of himself, one done by a great artist, true to life but yet more than that, elevated, drawn to his essence, almost godlike. I felt so happy, so radiant as he stood before me, I wanted to ask him if he'd come down to me from the heavens. Isn't that silly?

CHARIS: Oh, your Ladyship, that's just love. An overheated imagination.

ALCMENA: But, Charis, he kept making this jest, this peculiar joke, drawing a distinction between himself and Amphitryon, between my lover and my husband. If it hadn't come from my precious husband's own lips, I would have been offended.

CHARIS: Don't torment yourself. Didn't Amphitryon acknowledge the initial when you showed it to him today? It must be some alchemical property in the stone itself which tricks the eye. Yesterday we were at sixes and sevens, today things have returned to normal, and now we see them as they really are.

ALCMENA: What if he, like me, only glanced at the initial, and now when he returns with his witnesses, who will swear he never left the camp, and has a second look at this jewel—then it will be evidence against me, this strange initial. Which means it's not a gift from him, or so he'll claim, and can I even be sure, given my uncertainty about who's who and what's what, that this is the same jewel I received from his hand yesterday?

CHARIS: Hush, now, here he comes. Let's clear up once and for all this monogram confusion.

*(*ALCMENA *and* CHARIS *step back as—)*

Scene Five

*(*JUPITER *enters.* CHARIS *exits as* ALCMENA *throws herself at his feet.)*

ALCMENA: My dearest darling husband, I throw myself on your mercy, and lay this jewel at your feet. If *you* gave me this stone, with the initial of another's name upon it, a man I do not know, then I'll kiss it and treasure it all my days, and weep hot tears of joy over it. But if you did not give me this gift, if you disavow it, disclaim it, know nothing about it, then let me die, and bury my everlasting shame with my defiled body.

JUPITER: Darling, what's come over you? Please get up, and leave this jewel in the dust if you like, if it upsets you so, only please compose yourself. Arise, and tell me what's the matter.

(ALCMENA *gets to her feet and dries her tears.)*

ALCMENA: Since observing this stranger's monogram—

JUPITER: Ah. A J—

ALCMENA: Exactly. A J, not an A—

JUPITER: Hmmm.

ALCMENA: —I no longer trust my own most intimate emotions. I begin to believe someone else appeared before me last night and shared my bed, not you. My dearest husband, I want you to put my doubts to rest.

JUPITER: Darling, how can that be? How could another have shared your bed? You, who carry only one man's face and features in your heart, forever. Any man you receive is transformed by the power of your love into Amphitryon.

ALCMENA: That is not exactly the unequivocal response I desire. Please tell me, Husband, by your own lips, was it you I made love with last night? Or not? Say who it was! Say who! Say who! Say who!

JUPITER: It was I. No matter who it was, it was I. Or me, as the case may be.

ALCMENA: Amphitryon—

JUPITER: Stay calm. All that you felt, all that you touched, everything that happened—was me. Whoever crossed your threshold, you received no one but me, sweet Alcmena, and the favors you bestowed upon me, I thank you for them and am forever in your debt.

ALCMENA: No. That's not good enough. A straight answer is all that I desire, and so farewell.

JUPITER: Farewell? What farewell? Where are you going?

ALCMENA: Farewell, forever, I might add.

JUPITER: Hang on, wait a minute—

ALCMENA: I'd like you to leave now—

JUPITER: But Darling—

ALCMENA: Go—

JUPITER: Light of my life—

ALCMENA: Go, go, go—

JUPITER: Apple of my eye—

ALCMENA: Get out of here, go now—

JUPITER: Listen to me—

ALCMENA: I'm not going to listen to you. I don't want to go on living unless I know in my heart of hearts that my conduct has been beyond reproach.

JUPITER: What're you saying? What crime have you committed? What law have you broken? My darling wife, whom I adore, all the devils in hell could do their best to besmirch your virtue—smear you with brimstone and splatter you with sin and never so much as mark your breast with a single blemish, my darling, so pure is your heart and so splendid your virtue.

ALCMENA: No, no, no, no, no. I have been so dreadfully deceived.

JUPITER: He was the one who was deceived, my darling!

ALCMENA: He? He, who?

JUPITER: If he imagined as you held him in your arms that you dreamed of anyone other than your beloved Amphitryon—

ALCMENA: Ah! So you admit it, shameful man! It *was* someone else! Oh, gods, now the two of us must part. Go—

JUPITER: The kiss you gave him has bound me to you now more firmly than all the love you've ever shown me—

ALCMENA: I cannot stay here. You will never see me darken the door of our palazzo again!

*(*ALCMENA *starts to run out.* JUPITER *grabs her.)*

JUPITER: Stay!

ALCMENA: Let me go!

JUPITER: You think you can escape my love?

ALCMENA: Amphitryon, I want to flee. Release me, Darling, let me go—

JUPITER: Where would you flee to?

ALCMENA: I swear, if you come after me, I will call down the wrath of the gods upon you—

JUPITER: Oh, you would, would you?

ALCMENA: Not only that, I'd sooner die than return to your bed, I'll tell you that.

JUPITER: It's time to clear the celestial cobwebs from your eyes. It was no mere mortal man who came to you last night, but Zeus himself, a/k/a Jupiter, God of Thunder and Lightning, father of all the gods.

ALCMENA: Excuse me. Who?

JUPITER: Jupiter. With a J.

ALCMENA: You're mad.

JUPITER: Jupiter, I say. Zeus, himself.

ALCMENA: The war has addled you.

JUPITER: Jupiter. No less than he appeared before you last night, and shared your bed.

ALCMENA: Now I've heard everything. If that doesn't take the alibi cake. *(Tearing up)* Oh. Oh. Oh. Now I get it. You're trying to distract me from my horrible mistake. That's very sweet of you, Amphitryon, and it moves me to tears—but it won't work. Go find yourself another wife, my darling, one who'll make you happy. Go—

JUPITER: My dear wife. Jupiter *was* with you last night. He must have been. Look— *(Re: monogram)* There's his name. His initial, anyway. This morning, didn't I move to give you this jewel, and open the sealed case only to find you already wearing it at your breast?

ALCMENA: It's true—

JUPITER: Who else could have deceived you so? It must have been Jupiter himself, disguised as Amphitryon. Who else could have tricked you, a married woman, into believing another man to be her husband?

ALCMENA: No one. It's just not possible.

JUPITER: No, it's not. The only way he could have gained access to your bedroom is to have stolen your husband's features and impersonated him.

ALCMENA: I suppose you're right. Well then, in that case, I guess I'm not to blame after all. Am I?

JUPITER: An honest mistake—

*(*ALCMENA *kisses* JUPITER, *happy.)*

JUPITER: My goddess!

ALCMENA: Oh, I am so happy to have you back again, Amphitryon, and to have cleared up this celestial confusion. As long as everything's back the way it was.

JUPITER: Absolutely. I wonder, though—

ALCMENA: What?

JUPITER: If you've made him mad.

ALCMENA: I certainly made you mad. You were awful to me this morning.

JUPITER: But I wonder if you've made Jupiter mad, provoked his divine wrath and so on, by forswearing him and returning to Amphitryon.

ALCMENA: How can you say that? Haven't I always worshipped Jupiter, given thanks to him for all my blessings, including you, my darling?

JUPITER: But how do you worship him—exactly?

ALCMENA: I confess, to keep myself entertained, and because the walls of the temple are so blank and so boring, and because I'm so easily distracted, as you know, Darling, I usually imagine him to look rather like you, my dear.

JUPITER: Ah, and that's the idolatry that made him mad, that compelled him to visit you in your husband's form.

ALCMENA: Oh, dear. Really?

JUPITER: In the future, when you worship him at his altar, you must think only of him, not me—otherwise, he'll come back.

ALCMENA: I swear, I will. I remember what he looked like, down to the last detail, and I promise I won't confuse the two of you ever again.

JUPITER: Every time you see his monogram upon this jewel, this—J—think only of Jupiter, recall him in all his splendor, remember the thrill that ran through your female self, remember how you received the jewel from his hand. And if your husband distracts you, ask him to leave you alone for an hour or so, so that you might compose yourself.

ALCMENA: I know what I'll do. In the morning, at the altar, I'll think only of Jupiter for an hour, and after that put him completely out of my mind for the rest of the day.

JUPITER: Splendid idea. But, just for argument's sake, if he now, in all his glory, were to come to you once again, how would you behave?

ALCMENA: What a dreadful moment that would be!

JUPITER: But you haven't even seen his immortal visage yet, Alcmena. Let me tell you. Your heart would leap up in delight! You'd feel fire for him, and nothing but ice for Amphitryon.

ALCMENA: I don't think so. No, never—

JUPITER: Yes, make no mistake about it, Alcmena, if he were to touch your soul this instant, you'd want to fly with him to Olympus, and stay there forever, I guarantee it.

ALCMENA: *(Shaking her head)* Oh, no, Amphitryon, if I could only have yesterday back, I'd spend it locked away from gods and heroes both, so that I wouldn't be taken in again.

JUPITER: Really? In spite of what you felt last night?

ALCMENA: Oh, yes. Last night was divine—but I'd trade it gladly for a chance to do it all over with my husband.

JUPITER: *(Aside)* Damn! I've fallen in love with her, but her love for me was an illusion after all.

ALCMENA: What's the matter? Are you upset?

JUPITER: You're telling me you'd deny him? Jupiter? Source of all joys on Earth? What if he needed your love? What if—for argument's sake—Olympus is a cheerless place, bereft of affection? What if he were lonely in his divine splendor, lonely and bored, with nothing to do all day but make mischief? What if he craved not the mere senseless adoration of nations, prostrate in the dust, the endless sacrifices and offerings, but the love of a real, live, flesh-and-blood woman?

ALCMENA: What if?

JUPITER: Would you deny him then?

ALCMENA: Far be it from me to shirk my sacred duty—

JUPITER: Yes—

ALCMENA: And yet I have to say, if the choice were really mine—

JUPITER: Yes—

ALCMENA: I'd give him my reverence, and save all my love for you, Amphitryon.

JUPITER: Let me put it another way. If I were to you like this god—

ALCMENA: If you? If you? Suddenly I feel this strange sensation once again. I don't know whether to fall on my knees before you or not. *(She goes into his arms.)* I'm so confused. Are you Jupiter? Or are you my husband? Who are you, anyway?

JUPITER: You decide. I am Amphitryon—

ALCMENA: *(Dreamily)* Amphitryon—

JUPITER: To you. But I ask you again. If Jupiter himself were to come to you again, descend from Olympus to make love to you, what would you do?

ALCMENA: I'd follow you anywhere. I mean, if you were Jupiter, I would not know where my Amphitryon was, so—

JUPITER: And what if Amphitryon appeared?

ALCMENA: You are torturing me. How can Amphitryon appear when I'm holding him now in my arms?

JUPITER: What if, instead of Amphitryon, you have Jupiter himself now in your embrace—

ALCMENA: Oh, no—

JUPITER: And you think he's Amphitryon—but suddenly the real Amphitryon appears. What would you do then? How would you feel? What would your heart say?

ALCMENA: If you were the god, and you held me in your arms, as you do now—and suddenly Amphitryon appeared— *(Pause)* —then I'd be sad, because I'd wish that he were the god, and you'd remain Amphitryon, which you are. Aren't you? Tell me you're my Amphitryon, and let's go back to bed—

JUPITER: Of course I am! Of course I am, my darling! I am Amphitryon, and no other! Sosia!

*(*SOSIA *and* MERCURY *appear.* JUPITER *gestures for* MERCURY *to get lost, and he disappears.)*

SOSIA: Sir!

JUPITER: My faithful servant! Alcmena has for love of me made peace with me once more.

SOSIA: Good news, Sire.

JUPITER: Let's have a feast! Summon the guests!

SOSIA: Guests?

JUPITER: Go back to camp and invite my captains to dine with us tonight—

SOSIA: But, Sir, that's a five-hour trip each way—

JUPITER: Then you'd better get going, hadn't you?

*(*ALCMENA *and* JUPITER *exit, arm in arm—)*

Scene Six

(—leaving SOSIA *alone.* CHARIS *enters, looks at* SOSIA *with new eyes.)*

CHARIS: *(Aside)* What's going on here? The gods have dallied within this very palazzo. And this one here, who passes for my husband Sosia, may in fact be one of the immortals. Mercury, maybe.

SOSIA: *(Aside)* Great Zeus himself, impersonating my master—

CHARIS: *(Aside)* Oh, shame, shame, shame on me for the way I treated him today. What if he is a god?

SOSIA: *(Aside)* Not bad. If you have to be impersonated by someone—

CHARIS: *(Aside)* I'd hate to be wrong about something like this. I guess I'll just have to put him to the test. *(To* SOSIA*)* Oh, Darling, why don't we kiss and make up, too?

SOSIA: Later. At the moment, I've other things to do.

CHARIS: What other things?

SOSIA: You heard him. Go back to camp, invite the captains, prepare the feast, yadayadayada—

CHARIS: Just a word before you go, my sweet husband.

SOSIA: My sweet husband? Okay. That's more like it. I'll loiter for a second or two—

CHARIS: Tell me, Darling. What do you make of all this business, gods visiting our humble palazzo, and all the rest?

SOSIA: It's a mess.

CHARIS: *(Aside)* I guess he's not from Olympus after all. *(To* SOSIA*)* I think it's an honor. Who'd ever dream of having guests like that?

SOSIA: Who needs 'em? Life's confusing enough, without getting the gods involved.

CHARIS: *(Aside)* Is he or isn't he? I just can't make up my mind.

SOSIA: You know, it's nice of you to speak so politely to me, and a welcome change from earlier, when you gave me such a tongue lashing—

CHARIS: A tongue lashing? Oh, Darling, you exaggerate, I didn't mean to speak harshly to you—

SOSIA: And threatening to be unfaithful—

CHARIS: Oh, that. That was a joke—

SOSIA: Well, I'm sick of it, do you hear me? I won't stand for it—

CHARIS: *(Aside)* Heavens! What's happening to me?

SOSIA: Talking of sweaty muscular young men—

CHARIS: *(Aside)* I'm melting at the sound of his voice—

SOSIA: Making mock of our solemn marriage vows—

CHARIS: *(Aside)* He's so forceful, so—so—*manly*. He can't possibly be my husband. *(Gasps)* He must be a god!

SOSIA: You know, I think I'd like rigatoni for dinner, with a little sausage on the side—

*(*CHARIS *throws herself at* SOSIA*'s feet.)*

CHARIS: Anything, Darling! Anything you want!

SOSIA: What are you doing?

CHARIS: Behold me grovel in the dust at your feet.

SOSIA: Is something wrong?

CHARIS: You are he! You are he!

SOSIA: I am who?

CHARIS: Why deny it? Take me!

SOSIA: What? Here?

CHARIS: I saw it! I saw the fire in your eyes, the far-reaching flame of bright Apollo! Take me!

SOSIA: Sorcery! The gods have doubled you, too! One of you calls me a dirty dog, and the other one calls me a god! And I'm neither, I'm just Sosia, the same old jackass I've always been.

*(*SOSIA *exits.* CHARIS *picks herself up, disappointed.)*

CHARIS: Shoot. My husband, after all. I'm so disappointed. I saw the way my lady looked at breakfast this morning. I'd like a little taste of that ambrosia myself. Well, Sosia the jackass. It's a good thing I found out now, instead of *after*. No rigatoni and sausage for you, pal. *(She exits.)*

END OF ACT TWO

ACT THREE

Scene One

*(*AMPHITRYON*, discovered in front of his palazzo)*

AMPHITRYON: My captains! How I hate their valedictory congratulations and hearty hugs and handshakes. There's not one of my so-called cohorts I can confide in. *(Puzzles)* That a jewel can be stolen from a sealed box without breaking the seal—agreed. After all, a charlatan, a mountebank, a magician, a sleight-of-hand artist can all, from a distance, pull watches from pockets and coins from purses, and white rabbits from silken top hats, and cause pigeons to appear where last were seen bouquets of tulips. But to steal a man's shape and aspect, and use the theft to lay with his wife—now there's a *nasty* trick. What will they think of next? Instead of trusting our own good senses, and identifying our spouses by sight and sound and smell and touch, I suppose husbands will have to be branded and belled, like milk cows. *(Ponders)* I don't believe Alcmena's capable of colluding in such a deception. She must be mad. Insane. Tomorrow I'll surely have to send for a physician. I hate to wait until then— *(As he ponders—)*

Scene Two

*(—*MERCURY *enters, above, on the balcony.)*

MERCURY: I'm not fond of old Jupiter's scheme. The prospect of following in his hairy footsteps and playing the husband to the lady's maid Charis, as Jupiter has done with lovely Alcmena, fills me with ennui, frankly. Bores me to tears. I prefer to choose my own amusements. *(Sees* AMPHITRYON*)* Now this looks promising. Why don't I just drive this jealous fellow down here to distraction?

*(*AMPHITRYON *tries the doors; they're locked. He pounds on them in frustration.)*

AMPHITRYON: Now, why the devil are these doors locked in broad daylight?

MERCURY: Hey! Who's down there banging on the doors?

AMPHITRYON: *(Sees who it is)* It's me.

MERCURY: Me who?

AMPHITRYON: It's me, Sosia! Open up!

MERCURY: Why should I? Who are you and what do you want, and what gives you the right to talk to me in such an imperious manner?

AMPHITRYON: *(Incredulous)* You mean to say you don't know me?

MERCURY: Am I supposed to know every peddler and vagrant? Every hobo who bangs on these doors, looking for a handout or a hot meal? Go away—

AMPHITRYON: *(Aside)* I swear all of Thebes has been drinking absinthe, or smoking opium, or has been bitten by rabid dogs. It's most peculiar. *(To* MERCURY*)* Sosia, you know very well who I am! Open the damn door! So? So? So open the doors, and quit clowning around.

MERCURY: I'm tired of talking to you. I've got better things to do. Ciao! *(He starts to go.)*

AMPHITRYON: Come back here! *(He pounds on the doors some more.)* Open the damn doors, you good-for-nothing! Sosia!

(MERCURY *comes back.)*

MERCURY: Sirrah, if you don't quit causing such a ruckus, I'll have you beaten to a bloody pulp, tarred and feathered, and run out of town on a rail, for good measure.

AMPHITRYON: How dare you! How dare you talk that way to me!

MERCURY: *(Aside)* My, if looks could kill—

AMPHITRYON: You'd better stop this mutinous nonsense this minute, before you accumulate a backlog of more blows than you can absorb in one lifetime. Now come downstairs and open the damn doors!

MERCURY: Oh? And if I open the doors—who is it you wish to see?

AMPHITRYON: That's none of your damned business, you mangy mutt—

(MERCURY *howls like a dog, and laughs at himself.)*

MERCURY: You know something? I think you'd better run along now. You're really beginning to bore me.

AMPHITRYON: *(Spluttering)* Oh, I am, am I?! Wait'll I get my hands on you, I'll kick you to kingdom come for your impudence! You'll find out the hard way what happens to insolent servants who mock their masters.

MERCURY: Masters? You're my master?

AMPHITRYON: I am. Now you're going to deny you have a master, I suppose.

MERCURY: Not at all. I have only one master. And his name is—Amphitryon—

AMPHITRYON: Ah ha!

MERCURY: And when I tell him how you've carried on, disturbing the peace and so on, boy are you gonna get it!

AMPHITRYON: I am Amphitryon, you moron, none other, can't you see? Don't you recognize me?

MERCURY: *(Looks him over)* I don't think so.

AMPHITRYON: I am Amphitryon, I tell you.

MERCURY: Sure, and I'm a Greek god. Tell me, friend. How many snooks did you have down at the tavern? What's your poison, pal? Beer, wine, mead, or some of that awful retsina? That must be your problem. I'm told the tar content can drive the habitual retsina user mad. I feel sorry for you, Sirrah. Retsina's a nasty hangover. Go and sleep it off. And please don't bang on the doors any more. Amphitryon, the great Theban general with whom you have somehow confused your pathetic self, is inside taking a siesta, and I'd hate for you to disturb his rest.

AMPHITRYON: What? What did you say? Amphitryon's within?

MERCURY: Sure enough, he and his lovely—and if I may say so—*sensual* bride, Alcmena, have just laid down again for their afternoon—how shall I put it—tête-à-tête. So please, go away. You wouldn't want to disturb the happy couple, would you? Unless you want him to come out here and box your ears, *but good.* Take it from one who knows. You don't want him to box your ears— (He gives him a big smile and retires within, leaving—

Scene Three

*(—*AMPHITRYON *to tear his hair.)*

AMPHITRYON: Oh, unlucky man! What a mortal blow! I'm crushed, I'm done for! I'm buried, and my widow is already married to another, who takes my name and property! Not to mention my palazzo! Well, what have I got to lose? Nothing! Revenge is all that I have left to me. And a burning desire to see that that traitor Sosia is stewed alive in his own treacherous gravy! Under a *slow* fire!

(AMPHITRYON hears the approach of several people, draws back as—)

Scene Four

(—SOSIA enters, with a CAPTAIN.)

SOSIA: Here he is, Sir. All the captains I could round up at such short notice. I'm sorry it's not more of a crowd—

AMPHITRYON: There you are, you dirty dog!

SOSIA: Dog, Sir?

AMPHITRYON: You're a dog, and you'll die like a dog—

SOSIA: Oh, dear. What doglike thing have I done now, Sire, that you should want me dead?

AMPHITRYON: Don't play the fool with me! You know very well what you've done, you, you insolent cockroach! Now you'll find out who I really am—

SOSIA: I know who you are, you're my lord and master, Amphitryon—

AMPHITRYON: Oh! So you *do* know. Traitor! Worthless cur! Scoundrel! *(He draws his sword.)* Prepare to be skewered!

(SOSIA cowers behind the CAPTAIN.)

SOSIA: Oh, help me, Captain, help me! He's gone mad!

CAPTAIN: *(Restraining* AMPHITRYON*)* Forgive me, General—

AMPHITRYON: Don't touch me, or I will run you through, too! Now, out of my way, and let me have at this little mongoose! This wombat! This weasel! This centipede! This piece of carrion pie! This two-legged plate of steaming entrails!

SOSIA: Well, if you're going to kill me, Sir, please at least tell me why—

CAPTAIN: I'd like to know the reason myself, Sir. Surely the condemned man deserves to hear the details of his crime—

SOSIA: That doesn't seem so much to ask—

AMPHITRYON: I'll tell you then. Just moments ago, this *residue* scraped from the bottom of my boot, refused to unlock the door of mine own palazzo and, in spite of my repeated entreaties, kept it locked in my face, and then had the unmitigated gall to hurl down a series of insults, each one worse than the last, and any one of which was more than enough to get him hanged in any city in Greece, Thrace, or Anatolia—and finally, this frog spawn, this whale dreck, this bottom feeder, had the temerity to tell me that my wife was cosseted in my own bedroom with another man.

SOSIA: Cosseted?

AMPHITRYON: Die, mongrel!

*(*AMPHITRYON *stabs at* SOSIA, *who falls to his knees and covers his eyes and shrieks.)*

SOSIA: Oh heavens! I'm dead already! Help! Captain, help!

CAPTAIN: Calm yourself, General!

SOSIA: Is he still waving that sword around with such reckless abandon?

AMPHITRYON: Out of the way, I say! He must pay the ultimate price for the shame he's caused me—

SOSIA: But how could I have done you wrong when I've been in camp all day, following your orders and inviting people to dinner?

AMPHITRYON: What orders?

SOSIA: Your orders, Sir, to round up your captains and invite them to a feast.

AMPHITRYON: When did I give these orders?

SOSIA: Right after you reconciled with Alcmena—

AMPHITRYON: WHAT?

SOSIA: You were so overjoyed you gave orders for a great feast, told me to go back to camp and invite the captains—

CAPTAIN: It's true, Sir, he's been with me lo these past few hours, and never out of my sight.

AMPHITRYON: Oh, heavens! Every hour drags me deeper into the labyrinth. What am I to make of this, my friend? Did you hear what he said?

CAPTAIN: If it's a tissue of lies, Sir, it's easily enough cut through.

AMPHITRYON: And for that, I'll need your help. I am on fire to solve this mystery, even though I dread its eventual solution. Come! *Corragio! (He bangs on the doors with the butt of his sword. Suddenly the doors open—)*

Scene Five

*(—*JUPITER *comes out, in high dudgeon.)*

JUPITER: What's the ruckus? What wild rumpus requires me to come down from my conjugal bower to squelch this infernal racket? *(Sees the* CAPTAIN*)* Captain! Welcome!

(The AMPHITRYON ,CAPTAIN, *and* SOSIA *stare at* JUPITER.*)*

AMPHITRYON: Ye gods! My mirror image! Am I Narcissus?!?

CAPTAIN: What do I see? Two Amphitryons—

SOSIA: Count 'em. Two—

CAPTAIN: As alike as perfect twins, and no human eye can tell the difference between them.

AMPHITRYON: Ah, now the riddle's solved. And my blood runs cold at the answer—

CAPTAIN: Which one is Amphitryon, then? The real Amphitryon? My general? The master of this palatial palazzo?

*(*SOSIA *looks from one to the other.* AMPHITRYON *glowers;* JUPITER *smiles kindly.* SOSIA *makes his decision.)*

SOSIA: Sir, this one— *(Re:* JUPITER*)* —is Amphitryon, my master. This other— *(Re:* AMPHITRYON*)* —a rude, ill-tempered, mean-spirited imposter.

AMPHITRYON: Why, you little rat! You betray me once again!

*(*SOSIA *goes and stands by* JUPITER.*)*

CAPTAIN: *Incroyable! (Re:* AMPHITRYON*)* I would have sworn on my mother's grave you were my courageous commanding officer—

AMPHITRYON: And so I am, I swear! Oh, enough of this sorcery! *(Drawing his sword)* I'm going to put an end to this folderol once and for all—

CAPTAIN: *(Restraining him)* Stop!

AMPHITRYON: Unhand me, Sir! I'm going to puncture this infernal deceit! I'm going to open it up for all to see!

JUPITER: Calm down. There's no need for swordplay. I must say, a man so quick to defend his identity must have good reason to be anxious about it—

SOSIA: That's what I say. *(Re:* AMPHITRYON*)* He's got himself up to look like the master, padding and makeup and false eyebrows and so on, but it's not all that convincing when you look closely.

AMPHITRYON: You traitor! You'll pay for this! I'll flay you from head to toe! I'll boil you alive in olive oil!

SOSIA: Ho, ho, ho! My compassionate and kindly master won't stand for anyone laying so much as a finger on his favorite servant, will you?

JUPITER: Wouldn't dream of it—

SOSIA: —so don't you threaten me, you big galoot.

AMPHITRYON: Let me at him! Let me at him, I say! I'll skewer him on the spot!

CAPTAIN: Excuse me, Sir, we can't allow this dispute to escalate any further—Amphitryon versus Amphitryon—you must pull yourself together.

AMPHITRYON: Is this the help you offered me? Is this how you repay my valiant leadership? Is this how you follow me into battle?

CAPTAIN: Before I can follow you, Sir, first I must decide which of you is you.

AMPHITRYON: I am Amphitryon—

CAPTAIN: Very well, Sir, but so is he. Since the sword blade cannot make this determination with reason and discernment, perhaps it'd be better off back in its scabbard.

AMPHITRYON: Oh, very well— *(He reluctantly sheathes his sword.)*

CAPTAIN: Now, let us investigate this conundrum calmly. And each of you can make your case.

AMPHITRYON: Case?

CAPTAIN: To prove who you are.

AMPHITRYON: Absurd. Ridiculous. Prove who I am? How am I to do that? Everyone knows I am Amphitryon. I've always been Amphitryon—

JUPITER: Quite right, Captain. The proper way to go about settling this dispute is to listen to us both, and make your judgment. I promise to abide by the result. I believe, when you've heard my argument, that all of Thebes— *(Re:* AMPHITRYON*)* —and even this absurd and rank imposter—will acknowledge my suzerainty—

SOSIA: Suzerainity? What's suzerainity?

JUPITER: Over this army, and this palazzo, and these fields and vineyards, and the lady mistress, the lovely Alcmena, who reigns within, and quietly commands throughout these rooms—and concede all are mine, and no other's. The whole world shall know that no shame has befallen Amphitryon or his bride, and as for the suspicions that this fool here has himself aroused by his crude impersonation, here I stand, ready to dispel all doubts. Over dinner. So please come and make yourselves at home—

SOSIA: That settles it. Sir, the real Amphitryon is the one who now commands you to dine within. I don't know about all of you, but I'm famished—

AMPHITRYON: Oh heavens! Has any man ever been so thoroughly humiliated? To be robbed of my wife, my honor, my good name, and all my property by a most consummate trickster! While my friend here deserts me!

CAPTAIN: Patience, Sir! Hold your horses for a few more hours, yet, and all will be revealed, one way or another.

AMPHITRYON: Fair-weather friend! Go dine with the Great Pretender. I still have other allies besides you. You're not the only oyster in the stew. There are still men in Thebes who will stand by my side and help me take my revenge.

JUPITER: Go ahead. Call on them. I'll wait for their arrival. In fact, we'll set a place for them at the table—

AMPHITRYON: By Jove, by Jupiter, see if I don't bring back the entire citizenry of Thebes, before you have a chance to slip away. I'll be back, to reduce you to a mound of rubble, a paltry pile of bones, bleaching away in the midday sun— *(He exits—)*

Scene Six

(—leaving JUPITER, SOSIA, *and the* CAPTAIN.*)*

JUPITER: Well, then, Sir, come in and dine with us. You honor our table with your presence.

CAPTAIN: I don't know about you, but my head is spinning. I'm completely flummoxed. This whole matter of twin Amphitryons is an inscrutable pancake, as my mother used to say.

SOSIA: Well, put your incredulity on hold, and what say we go in and carouse until the cows come home?

JUPITER: Captain—
(The CAPTAIN *follows* JUPITER *into the palazzo—)*

Scene Seven

(—leaving SOSIA *alone for the moment.)*

SOSIA: I think I'll join them at the big table. I'm eager to spin a tale or two of the war, even though I missed most of it, hiding in the tent—but what the hell, I can swap lies with the best of them, and I have to say, I'm so hungry, I could eat a horse! *(He starts in, just as—)*

Scene Eight

*(—*MERCURY *enters.* SOSIA *groans.)*

SOSIA: Uh-oh.

MERCURY: Where do you think you're going?

SOSIA: In to dinner?

MERCURY: I don't think so. Be off, before I have to be severe with you.

SOSIA: Oh, please, most magnificent and magnanimous me, have mercy on your lesser self. Take it easy on Sosia, Sosia. Why do you always want to beat yourself about the head and shoulders so?

MERCURY: So you're up to your usual shenanigans, huh? Stealing my name again?

SOSIA: Oh, no, no, no, I wouldn't think of it. My name's worth nothing to me. Take half of it. Sos. Ia. Or all of it, for that matter. After all, aren't we two peas in a pod? As alike as Castor and Pollux? Romulus and Remus? Frick and Frack? Let those two Amphitryons tear each other to pieces! Why shouldn't Sosia and Sosia sit down together like the lion and the lamb and share a fraternal jug of wine, a loaf of bread, and drink to our mutual well-being and longevity? What'd you say?

MERCURY: No thank you. I don't wish to share.

SOSIA: Just let me be your shadow, then—

MERCURY: Not even my footprint in the sand!

SOSIA: You are a hard-hearted person!

MERCURY: Haven't I earned my supper tonight? Didn't I walk all the way from camp last night to do my master's bidding? Didn't I go back to camp to round up the captains for this evening's dinner? Don't I deserve a little rest? I'm weary. My dogs are barking, let me tell you. We're having rigatoni and sausage for supper, by the way—

SOSIA: So Charis made rigatoni and sausage after all—

MERCURY: But not for you. Yum yum yum. Eat your heart out.

SOSIA: Oh, good. I'll just crawl off in a corner and die. Rigatoni, you say?

MERCURY: Fresh, home-made—

SOSIA: I hope you choke on it. *(Aside)* It's really too much. More than a poor man can stand—

MERCURY: Button your lip, little man. And make yourself scarce.

*(*MERCURY *goes in, leaving—)*

Scene Nine

(—a very hungry SOSIA *behind.)*

SOSIA: I hope your dinner turns out to be a dog's breakfast, I really do. Overbearing swine. Ooo. Am I hungry. *(Sniffs)* Something smells wonderful—

(The doors swing open and—)

Scene Ten

*(*CHARIS *enters, with an empty pot. She does a doubletake when she sees* SOSIA.*)*

CHARIS: How did you get out here so fast? Didn't I just leave you bellied up to the dinner table?

SOSIA: Well, I—

CHARIS: You are very quick this evening. Wolfing down my cooking like there was no tomorrow—

SOSIA: Did I enjoy it?

CHARIS: You loved it. Every delectable bite.

SOSIA: It was delicious?

CHARIS: Scrumptious. Incomparable.

SOSIA: No kidding.

CHARIS: So good it made you want to slap your mama.

SOSIA: That good?

CHARIS: So you told me. *(Coquettishly)* I don't mind you devouring my rigatoni in a single gulp. After all, you worked—*hard*—today—

SOSIA: Didn't I—

CHARIS: And you weren't the least bit—quick—this evening, before supper.

SOSIA: I wasn't?

CHARIS: Oh, no, darling, not at all— *(She gives him a big kiss, pats his bottom, and starts off.)*

SOSIA: Where're you going?

CHARIS: To buy more sausage. You said you wanted seconds—

SOSIA: Oh, yes—

CHARIS: Then go back in and cool your heels, Darling—

SOSIA: Darling—

CHARIS: And just wait until you taste the bread pudding souffle I've made you for dessert—

SOSIA: Bread pudding souffle—

CHARIS: With whiskey sauce—

SOSIA: *(Gulps weakly)* Served piping hot?

CHARIS: One bite, and you won't want to eat it—you'll want to sit on it.

*(*CHARIS *exits.* SOSIA *looks after her wistfully, and then at the doors.)*

SOSIA: Oh, no— *(He sighs.)* Oh, my goodness. Here's the imposter again, and he's collected quite a crowd—

Scene Eleven

*(*AMPHITRYON *enters, with an officer, as a crowd of citizens mutters and seethes offstage.)*

AMPHITRYON: Citizens of Thebes! Who am I?

OFFSTAGE CITIZENS: Amphitryon!

AMPHITRYON: Say it again!

OFFSTAGE CITIZENS: Amphitryon!

AMPHITRYON: You know, that's got a ring to it. Rolls right off the tongue. *(To* COLONEL*)* Now when the other appears, the one who would steal me from my wife's affections, and separate me from my very name, and obliges you to choose between us, even though, through his sorcery we look alike as two drops of water on a windowpane, remember that I'm Amphitryon.

OFFSTAGE CITIZENS: Okay, we will, we won't forget, you bet!

COLONEL: I don't need to be reminded who you are. As for trials and judgments and contests, I say to hell with that! Let's run the bastard through. Kill 'em all, and let the gods sort 'em out, that's my motto.

AMPHITRYON: Then let's go in, and do just that.

(SOSIA throws himself at AMPHITRYON's feet.)

SOSIA: Master!

AMPHITRYON: What now?

SOSIA: I've changed my mind! I believe you are he, and he not you. For my doubts and bad judgment, I deserve to die! Bury me alive, I won't make a sound, I swear it. Only please forgive me for my mendacity—

AMPHITRYON: Get up, and tell me what has happened to change your mind.

SOSIA: Well, they wouldn't let me come in to dinner, that's the main thing, and I'm famished. The other me, who's in league with the other you, barred my way, and told me to stop being Sosia, on pain of death. And frankly, I'm sick of it.

AMPHITRYON: You see? My servant is bewitched in the same way I am.

COLONEL: It's a plague.

SOSIA: Citizens of Thebes! This is the real Amphitryon, the one who stands before you now. Colonel, if you would be so kind as to storm the house, and slaughter the inhabitants, there may still be some sausage and rigatoni left. If we hurry—

COLONEL: My pleasure. Sire?

AMPHITRYON: Follow me, my friend.

(They start for the doors. The doors swing open, and—)

SOSIA: Look! There they are now!

Scene Twelve

(—ALCMENA, CHARIS, JUPITER, and MERCURY enter.)

JUPITER: Citizens of Thebes! Welcome to my palazzo!

AMPHITRYON: Prepare to meet your maker—

JUPITER: Vice versa, I assure you.

COLONEL: Astonishing! This must be witchcraft! Will wonders never cease!

JUPITER: You must show the entire world, my love, that no one has touched you but your own husband, Amphitryon.

ALCMENA: And no one has! I know it in my heart!

(AMPHITRYON *steps forward.)*

AMPHITRYON: Then which one of us, Madame, do you accept?

ALCMENA: Well, I—oh, dear. There are two of you now, aren't there? This is most distressing—

COLONEL: Declare yourself, Princess, you must choose between them.

AMPHITRYON: Alcmena, light of my life! If you say you accept that man standing there as your husband, then before you can finish the thought, I will fall upon this sword and solve this riddle for you.

ALCMENA: Please—

AMPHITRYON: Don't tell me you don't know this voice, this face, this heart which beats only for love of you, these lips which have kissed you a thousand times a thousand times?

ALCMENA: Oh, I wish I were anywhere but here—Hades even!

AMPHITRYON: You see, citizens? She will not declare for that man! Pachyderms will walk on water before she declares that man her husband!

COLONEL: But still she hesitates. Princess! Pronounce! Speak one word, and I'll have the imposter's head on a pike!

JUPITER: Darling, you must speak the truth. The citizens demand it.

ALCMENA: Citizens— *(Hesitates)* Amphitryon— *(Re:* JUPITER*)* —is here beside me.

AMPHITRYON: WHAT? HE? AMPHITRYON? I AM UNDONE!

COLONEL: So be it, she has spoken—

AMPHITRYON: But Alcmena—

COLONEL: Go now, get out of town, imposter, before I'm obliged to cut off your head and impale it at the nearest intersection—

AMPHITRYON: Don't be hasty. My darling—

ALCMENA: You dare speak to me that way? With my husband, in all his radiance, beside me? What did I ever do to you that you should disturb my life this way? Oh, I was misled and confused, and for awhile could not tell the two of you apart, but now it's obvious. Compared to my beloved, you are rank and gross, and odious and offensive to my sight. You succeeded for a time in your vile deception, and have sullied my reputation and my marriage bed and nearly ruined my life—are you happy? Go! Go and leave me alone. *(To* JUPITER*)* Husband, let me go in now, and lie down. I have such a headache. This is the worst hour of my life. Now all of Thebes knows how I was cozzened by this man, how he had his vile way with me—

JUPITER: Wait a moment, my beauty! You are about to be vindicated, your honor restored—intact. *(To* AMPHITRYON*)* Do you believe now that I'm Amphitryon?

AMPHITRYON: I believe you're not Amphitryon, and never will be—

ALCMENA: Stubborn man—

COLONEL: You deny it still, you dirty dog? Are you calling the princess a liar?

AMPHITRYON: No. Every word she's said is true. I'd stake my life on this: that he is indeed, in every way, Amphitryon to her.

JUPITER: Good answer. You *are* Amphitryon, after all.

AMPHITRYON: Then who are you?

JUPITER: Amphitryon, also. I thought you knew.

AMPHITRYON: Speak so we can understand you. My head swims with confusion.

JUPITER: You really want to know? I am Amphitryon—and every other creature under heaven, should I so choose—

(JUPITER *gestures. Thunder and lightning and smoke. When the smoke clears,* JUPITER *is holding a thunderbolt.)*

OFFSTAGE CITIZENS: *(Shouts and cries)* Jupiter!

COLONEL: Oh my god! It's great Jupiter himself!

ALCMENA: Oh! Mercy!

*(*ALCMENA *swoons, and falls into* AMPHITRYON*'s arms.)*

JUPITER: In your house, Jupiter has been—happy. Content. So pack up your cares and woes and let your mind be clear and your heart be light. None of these events will do you any lasting harm, but only redound to your good fortune and reputation. Both you and your lovely wife have acquitted yourselves admirably. In fact, as a token of my divine gratitude, I will grant you your fondest, most heart-felt wish.

AMPHITRYON: A son. I'd like a son.

JUPITER: And you shall have one. And his name shall be Hercules, and he'll be half-god, half-man, I hope you don't mind.

AMPHITRYON: I'm not wild about the idea—

*(*JUPITER *glowers.)*

AMPHITRYON: But what can I do about it?

JUPITER: Nothing.

AMPHITRYON: In that case, I accept. My thanks.

ALCMENA: And mine!

JUPITER: Farewell, divine Alcmena, loveliest of mortal women. Think of me. Mercury—

MERCURY: Right behind you, Boss—

CHARIS: Ciao!

MERCURY: See you, Sweetie—

(They disappear in a wonderful stage effect.)

CHARIS: Sigh.

*(*ALCMENA *embraces* AMPHITRYON.*)*

ALCMENA: Amphitryon!

AMPHITRYON: Alcmena!

ALCMENA: Is it really you?

AMPHITRYON: It is!

ALCMENA: Darling!

*(*ALCMENA *and* AMPHITRYON *kiss—)*

ALCMENA: I'm pregnant!

AMPHITRYON: We'll work it out.

(— and go in.)

CHARIS: Sosia?

SOSIA: Charis!

CHARIS: Is it really you?

SOSIA: It's true. It's me.

CHARIS: Oh, well.

*(*CHARIS *and* SOSIA *kiss.)*

SOSIA: I'm starving.

CHARIS: Go in the house. I'll see what I can scrounge up for supper.

SOSIA: Sausage and rigatoni?

CHARIS: Fat chance.

(SOSIA goes in.)

COLONEL: I suppose things are back to normal now, just the way they were before the strange and wonderful events that lately have occurred here in sacred and picturesque Thebes.

(CHARIS gives the COLONEL a speculative once over.)

CHARIS: *Au contraire*, Colonel. Once the gods have stirred the pot, things are never the same afterwards. Never—

(CHARIS smiles amorously, as the COLONEL smiles, too—and the lights fade—)

END OF PLAY

www.ingramcontent.com/pod-product-compliance
Lightning Source LLC
Chambersburg PA
CBHW061043050726
47592CB00004B/1575

* 9 7 8 0 8 8 1 4 5 1 2 7 6 *